Steps In Human Progress

by

Christian D. Larson

Steps In Human Progress
by Christian D. Larson

Copyright © 2023

All Rights reserved.

ISBN: 978-93-59394-67-1

Published by

DOUBLE 9 BOOKS

2/13-B, Ansari Road
Daryaganj, New Delhi – 110002
info@double9books.com
www.double9books.com
Tel. 011-40042856

ABOUT THE AUTHOR

Living between 1874 and 1954, Christian Daa Larson emerged as a leader and educator within the American New Thought community. The pioneering figure, Horatio Dresser, hailed Larson as one of the originators of the New Thought movement. Larson's literature, even centuries later, remains in circulation. In fact, his works even influenced significant writers and experts in the field of New Thought, such as Religious Science founder Ernest Holmes. Larson's birthplace of Forrest City, Iowa, was where his Norwegian parents resided. Iowa State College and Meadville Theological School in Pennsylvania were attended by him, as well as his brother Fenwicke Holmes, who also took a correspondence course with Larson at the Unitarian theological school. Larson's The Ideal Made Real was thought of on the same level as Ralph Waldo Trine's In Tune with the Infinite, according to Fenwicke's account in Ernest Holmes: His Life and Times. His ideas greatly impacted Ernest, and Fenwicke goes into further detail about this.

CONTENTS

Steps to the Higher Self 7

Steps to Higher Truths...21

Steps to the Spiritual 36

Steps to the Higher Self

In the presence of modern thought and aspiration what may we consider the greatest, the worthiest, the most important and the most inspiring thing that man can do. This is one of the leading questions of today, and we are face to face with a new answer, an answer that has never been given before. In the fields of invention, art, discovery, music, literature, industrial achievement and special mental attainment, man has accomplished much, and he will, in all these fields, accomplish vastly more. But there is another field, the most important that was ever known, which we are about to enter; and it is in this new field that man will do his greatest work — work, indeed, that will cause the wonder works of history to pale into utter insignificance.

The age of real wonders has just begun. The next one hundred years will witness achievements so extraordinary that the terms "marvelous" and "miraculous" will not begin to describe them. Everything that the master minds of today are dreaming about will be realized, and infinitely more. Even much of what can now be discerned in the light of the soul's vision will come to pass, and hundreds of worlds, as yet closed to the minds of the many, will open their limitless possibilities to the race. Accordingly, the welfare, the happiness and the progress of man will be promoted as never before. All these things, however, will simply mark the continuation of lines of progress already in action; they will naturally follow the further development of fields that are well known, and therefore will not necessarily be the result of a new step in advancement. But man is on the verge of a new step. Among all the known wonders there is a new wonder, far greater than all the others, just appearing at the dawn of the new day, and it heralds the next step in the progress of the world.

Thus far human attainments and achievements have concerned themselves principally with things, and with those mental faculties that act directly upon things; and the reason why is found in the fact that we have understood only those forces in man that can be applied to things. But the coming of modern metaphysics and the new psychology has opened our minds to the consciousness and the understanding of other forces — higher and more powerful forces — forces that can be applied to elements that are above things, in brief, the creative elements within man himself. In the past, the various steps in progress have been taken in those worlds that lie outside of the being of man; but the next step will be taken in those worlds that lie *within* the being of man. The next step in human progress will be to gain complete mastery over the creative forces and the creative elements within the human personality so that we can transform our interior nature and our personal appearance into what may be termed an Edition de Luxe of man.

Men and women are something like books — all kinds of editions, all styles of binding and every imaginable subject introduced in the contents; but there is one difference. Among books we find editions that have quality, richness and Worth, both as to contents and general appearance. The subject matter in some of these books constitutes the very essence of inspirational power, while the physical appearance is all that high art can cause it to be. Among people, however, it is almost impossible to find rich interior quality and rare personal appearance combined in the same person. The finest characters and the greatest minds do not always dwell in beautiful personalities, while persons who are exceptionally attractive to physical sight do not always possess unlimited riches of mind and soul. True, there are exceptions to all general rules; but the fact remains that Editions de Luxe of the being of man have not as yet appeared. However, if we can have Editions de Luxe of books we can have Editions de Luxe of men and women. Man has the inherent power to do far more with himself than he ever did with things; and the next step in his progress is to learn how.

When we look at the human family we find any number of paper editions, cheap cloth editions and the like; although occasionally we find a few that approach something far better, and it is the psychological study of the creative elements that are active in the personal natures of these few that has given us the secret to the next step in human progress. What one person can do, all can learn to do; what a few have accomplished more or less unconsciously, all can learn to accomplish consciously and intelligently. And where unconscious action has, under favorable conditions, produced results to a certain degree, intelligent action can, under any condition, produce results to the very highest degree. This is the law, and no law in life can ever fail when properly applied.

The reason why people who are extremely attractive physically are not always competent mentally or highly developed spiritually, is readily explained. When the creative process in the human system tends to build up and perfect the outer personality, nearly all the energy generated in the system will be used for that purpose, and in consequence there will be but a fraction remaining with which to build up mind and soul. In like manner, when the creative process tends to produce mental brilliancy, most of the energy of the system will be drawn into the mind, and the development of

the physical personality will necessarily be retarded. In some people we find
this energy dividing itself into several forces, one of which tends to build
up the personality, white the other tends to develop the various phases
of mind, character and soul. And this is the ideal arrangement; therefore
people who are built on these lines, are always attractive in body, brilliant
in mind, strong in character and beautiful in soul; that is, if they are well
supplied with energy and do not waste their forces in any form or manner.

When the creative energies of the system naturally divide themselves
among the various factors in human life, the greatest possible results are
not always produced in any one place of action; the reason being that in the
average person most of the energy generated in his system is wasted; and
if what remains is to be divided among several factors, the amount given
to each will be small. There is enough energy, however, generated in the
system to develop to the highest degree desired, everything that exists in
the entire being of man; therefore, when a person properly saves his energy
and applies it according to the laws of human development, he can secure
just as great results in all the factors of his being as is usually secured in but
one. In fact, he can do far better because he will act consciously, and will
personally control the laws through which results are to be gained.

When a person has learned to save all the forces in his system, and
has learned to personally control the creative elements of his being, he can
develop a more attractive personality than was ever seen before; he can
develop a more powerful and a more brilliant mind than was ever known
before; and he can develop the very highest states of character and soul that
the finest consciousness has ever discerned in the ideal. He can do all these
things at the same time; he has sufficient energy when he saves it all; and
what is so strongly in his favor is the great fact that when we develop the
whole man we secure greater results through any one part than we possibly
could if we developed that one part alone. In this connection it is well to
remember that no chain is stronger than its weakest link; but when every
fink is strong — exceptionally strong — the strength of the whole chain will
be great indeed.

There are many inspiring scenes in nature — scenes that lift the soul
to the very heights of empyrean realms; but the most inspiring scene of all
is the sight of a human personality that reveals, in visible form, all that is
pure, all that is rich, all that is high, all that is worthy, all that is beautiful
and all that is ideal in existence sublime. When we are in the presence of
a human personality where "the elements are so mixed" that we feel as if
we have met the very climax of workmanship divine, our thoughts of man
cease to dwell upon earth. Man, to us, is no longer a mere human creature;
he is something more, and we begin to gain glimpses of what can be done

with that "something more." And as those glimpses reveal the possibilities that He before us, we realize that we are beginning the study of the most interesting, the most profitable and the most fascinating theme that has ever presented itself to the mind of man.

When we meet people who express, even to a slight degree, the richness and the beauty that is inherent in human nature, we realize that we are in the very presence of the kings and queens of earth; and new faith is awakened within us. We no longer think of the human race as "depraved," or as "almost hopeless," or as "mere weaklings" of little more consequence than the leaf that comes with the wind, and with the same wind is blown away. We can see in man the Real Man; and as this Real Man appears before us in all his majesty and power, we begin to understand why "thou art mindful of him." We also begin to see, as never before, how much time and energy we have wasted in building up and tearing down useless things, while the greatest world of all worlds — the world within — has remained undeveloped and unexplored.

The greatest ambition of the coming day will be, not to write the best book, not to invent the most wonderful machine, not to paint the most inspiring picture, not to conduct the largest enterprise, not to amass the greatest amount of gold, but to develop and express the finest, the strongest, the most perfect, the most beautiful and the most inspiring personality in the world. To have the power to manipulate the creative elements in the world of things is truly a mark of greatness; but to exercise that same power upon the creative elements in human life is a mark of far greater greatness. And to enter this new field and develop the marvelous possibilities that are contained therein, is the next step in human progress.

We must remember, however, that to enter this new field is not to neglect other lines of progress and achievement. You may write an extraordinary book, or any number of them, and at the same time build and rebuild yourself, until you become an Edition de Luxe, both in human quality and in personal appearance. You may paint the most inspiring picture that the world has ever seen, and at the same time apply the divine art within your own being until you become the most inspiring living picture that the world has ever seen. You may conduct a great business enterprise and be a power in the world of practical things, and at the same time so direct the creative elements in your own being that you become as rich in personal quality as the possessions over which you exercise control; as noble in bearing as the kingship that rules in your mind; as strong in personal expression as the power that governs your vast domain; and as attractive in personal appearance as the richly adorned mansion you call your home. Whatever you do, you can become a genius in your sphere, and reach the highest places in practical achievement; but you can, at the same time, do even greater things with yourself. You can so rebuild and perfect your own personality that you become an Edition de Luxe in living, human form.

The personal worth of the man should at least be as great as the actual worth of his possessions; otherwise, he is not in keeping with his world. And his personal worth should be fully expressed through every atom in his being. He should 'Took" it in every sense of the term. The woman should at least be as beautiful as her gowns; otherwise, she is not true to the matchless charms of her nature. But this is but the beginning for her. The adorner's art is as nothing compared with the beautifying power that is latent in the feminine soul. People in general should at least be as attractive in themselves as are the houses they build or the surroundings in which they live. True, some are more attractive, but such attractiveness is born, not made. Henceforth, we must not depend on what we receive through heredity, but must proceed to make ourselves, and continue to remake ourselves until we become precisely what we wish to be. Nor is this a "mere dream" or a "useless desire." Man positively can remake himself according to his highest ideal of himself, and to do this will be the next step in his progress.

The purpose we have in mind is to consciously control and direct the creative elements in the system so as to rebuild the human personality according to our highest conception of what we personally should wish to be. These creative elements can be trained to act not only upon that finer field of fife that lies back of and within the personality, but also upon the tangible personality itself, even the cell-structures of the physical body. The use of these creative elements in furthering the purpose we have in view will, at first, result in a strong, attractive personality in man, and a beautiful, charming, fascinating personality in woman. But this is but the beginning; when man learns to control the building power that is inherent in his mind, and when woman learns to control the beautifying power that is in her soul, there is no ideal in connection with the perfecting of the human entity that cannot be realized. Then every individual may certainly become an Edition de Luxe, and according to his own ideal of what such an edition should be.

This new and wonderful goal, however, is to be reached, not by acting upon the personality from without, but by unfolding the strong, the beautiful and the ideal from within. The finer elements of mind, thought, feeling, consciousness and soul are to be given predominance in every action and phase of life. And when these elements are given the first place in all that pertains to actual living, they tend to work themselves out into actual expression through the personality. Thus the personality gradually changes from a state of weakness and inferiority to a state of richness, quality and high worth. You no longer present a "common" personal appearance; the ordinary has entirely disappeared from your life, and you become one of the "rare products" of creative art divine. In other words, you remove the cheap binding from your personal appearance; you remove the cheap paper, page after page, from your nature; you insert high art illumined pages instead, and you have your entire personal self bound in de Luxe.

Man has the power to remake himself and cause both his interior nature and his external appearance to become as far superior to the "average person" as the highly cultivated rose is superior to the weed. And the day is at hand to begin. We are now in possession of the necessary principles, the necessary methods and the necessary facts; we are ready for this next step in human progress; we are ready to remake ourselves in the image and likeness of our highest ideals, and thus become, in the true sense of the term, the crowning glory of Nature's sublime creative art.

The same power, the same efficiency, the same insight and the same genius that we have demonstrated in the world of things, we can now demonstrate in that world that is above things — the world of ideal human life; and we can cause everything that is ideal in that finer life to become ideal in actual, personal life. This finer life, and the world from which it springs, is within man; therefore, it cannot be acted upon through physical means; nor can it be reached through the channels of objective actions. To act upon that world subjective actions, applied through the elements of mind, thought, feeling, consciousness and soul, become necessary. That world, however, is almost wholly undeveloped; it is virgin soil, but its productive capacity is limitless. Rich rewards, therefore, are in store for those who will learn to cultivate the new fields of that vast domain. And anyone can learn to begin at once. Moreover, to be just to ourselves and the people with whom we come in contact, we must learn to begin at once.

The fact is that no person has the right to present a cheap, common, ordinary personal appearance to the world when he knows how to build in himself a superior personality. If we carry upon us a commonplace personal appearance, we invariably produce a cheap impression upon the mind of every person we meet; and cheap impressions lead to cheap thinking and inferior living. It may seem somewhat far-fetched, but it is the truth that every person who presents a cheap personal appearance tends to draw the race down into inferior thought and life. The idea, however, is not that every person, to produce good impressions upon others, must be elegantly dressed; dress does not constitute personal appearance; besides, it is those things that are alive — the *living appearance* — that produces the deepest impressions upon our minds. Dress as well as you possibly can; it is very important to do so, and remember, it is not the price of your clothes, but the way you wear them, that constitutes wholesome appearance. But dress is secondary; real personal appearance is in yourself, in your countenance, in your bearing, in your conduct, in your attitude, in your movements and in the general expression of your personal life. This being true, we all can have a fairly good and wholesome personal appearance, and when we learn to use the finer creative elements within us, this appearance may become extraordinary.

When you develop a superior personality, you become an inspiration to every person you meet; which fact we shall admit when we realize that a superior personality does not simply constitute a well-shaped physical form, but a refined, wholesome physical form, that is actually alive with the richest qualities and the highest states of sublime worth that can possibly be found in body, mind and soul. Shape is secondary; any shape becomes strong and attractive when alive with supreme power and high worth; and any shape becomes charmingly beautiful when animated with the very life, the very essence and the very soul of the beautiful. But the shape of any personal form can be so modified as to correspond exactly with the ideal personality we have undertaken to build. The human form is not only very plastic, but is constantly being reconstructed by the renewing forces in nature; therefore superior creative art from within will find no difficulty in remolding the personal form according to the finest pattern that we may have selected.

A beautiful woman, if she be truly beautiful in body, mind and soul, is doing more for the race than the richest and most liberal philanthropist. She is awakening those finer things in human life that alone can make living truly worth while. And every man who is in possession of a strong, attractive, wholesome, spirited personality, is leading hundreds, possibly thousands, to greater things. There is nothing that is more conducive to greater things than a human personality so constituted, that it tends to inspire in everybody a *living desire* to do greater things. And all men and women can exercise this inspirational power through their personal appearance as well as through their thoughts and deeds. These are facts, therefore it is not only what we think or say or do, but also "how we look," that determines our value to the race. But personal appearance has been ignored, or simply dealt with in the most superficial manner. An attractive personality has been looked upon as a luxury; now we know it to be a necessity. And the reason why is found in the fact that the power of appearance is one of the great powers in the world, not only in the life of the individual himself, but also in the life of every person that he may meet.

The world is governed by mental impressions, and everything we meet, in any manner whatever, produces a mental impression; but those impressions we gain from the people we meet are the strongest of all, and therefore exercise the greatest power upon our mode of life, thought and action. Happy, then, is the man whose personality gives only impressions of the strong, the worthy, the high, the superior, the beautiful and the ideal to every person that may come his way.

The foregoing facts prove conclusively that the next step in human progress is a necessity if we are to promote general progress as perfectly and as extensively as we would have the power to do if we could take advantage of all our present possibilities. But we cannot take advantage of all those possibilities so long as we, ourselves, continue to be, in many respects, an "inferior product." So long as the human personality produces inferior impressions upon the mind of the masses, the progress of mankind in general will be retarded. But, on the other hand, the more inspiring personalities we have in the world, the greater will become that power in the world that leads upward and onward. *And here is our opportunity.*

In taking this next step in human progress, however, we are not simply becoming benefactors. It is the individual who takes this next step who will realize the greatest gain. To prove this we might mention hundreds of incontrovertible facts, and shall at the outset present two of these, though these two are by no means the most important. First, we know that a man who has a strong, wholesome, attractive personality can accomplish fully twice as much, and more, with the same talent as the man who is personally weak, spiritless or unattractive. Second, we know that a woman who is beautiful in person, sweet in disposition and lovely in soul, can get almost anything she may want in this world. And there is a reason why — a reason that is not based upon selfish love, physical desire or personal vanity, but a reason that can only be found higher up in the finer life of ideal soul existence.

Should we have no other grounds upon which to base the value of this next step than the two great facts just presented, the subject before us would deserve all the time and attention that could be possibly given; but we are yet to look into the vast realms that this new step will open up to the mind, to the intellect, to the soul, to the fields of consciousness, to the physical senses and to all the faculties, functions, forces and elements in the entire being of man. In fact, the human world will be so enlarged, so enriched, so beautified and so perfected that the joy of living will be multiplied even hundreds of times.

We have found unlimited interest and fascination in exercising creative power in the world of things; we can imagine what our interest and fascination will be when we learn to exercise this creative power in the limitless domains of real human life; and also the supreme delight that we shall naturally enjoy when we begin to note results. Surely, we can think of no step in human progress that could add so richly to the happiness and the welfare of life as this next step before us; we shall therefore proceed with more interest and with more pleasure than we ever knew before.

To proceed, begin in the beginning; and the first essential is to picture in your mind your ideal of yourself. Then continue to see this ideal picture, no matter what external circumstances or conditions may be. You will daily grow more and more into the likeness of that picture until you become in the real what you have seen in the ideal. And the reason why is found in the fact that the energies of the system invariably select your predominating thought, or leading mental picture, as the pattern for their work. What you habitually *think* of yourself is your predominating thought of yourself; and it is this thought that your creative energies use as their model in building and rebuilding you. Therefore, when you improve your thought of yourself by picturing in your mind your highest ideal of yourself, your creative energies will have an improved model, and will, in consequence, begin to rebuild you according to the likeness of this new and better model. This is the basic principle in all human advancement, and there is absolutely no limit to its possibility and power. And as it is very easily applied by anyone, there is no reason why we all should not make a beginning now that will culminate in far greater results than we ever dreamed.

To picture in your mind that ideal of yourself that you wish to realize in personal form, it is necessary to incorporate in that picture every ideal quality that you can think of. The imagination governs completely all the creative forces of the system; therefore the imaging faculty must be trained to picture only those qualities and conditions that you wish to express in the new and improved personality.

To give all these ideal pictures predominance in consciousness, *live in* the consciousness of every ideal quality that you have begun to picture. This will so deepen the ideal in your life that all the elements of the ideal will become living elements throughout your being. You thus cause ideal qualities to become actual parts of your personality, and as you continue, you personally will be composed entirely of such qualities. When this is accomplished, you will have eliminated the cheap and the inferior from your personality, and the very cells in your body will have become as rich in texture as the petals of the highly cultivated rose.

When you have clearly formed in mind a complete picture of the new personality that you have begun to build, that is, when you can distinctly see yourself as you would actually appear after you had become an Edition de

Luxe in human form, live with a deep, constant desire to build and express such a personality. What you constantly desire to do, you will inspire your creative energies to do, but this desire must be so deep and so strong that it becomes, not only a permanent power, but a ruling power in your life. The entire system must continue in perfect health and in perfect harmony. When the health is not perfect, the natural building processes of the system are interfered with, and it is not possible to build the strong, the beautiful and the ideal without perfect harmony.

To eliminate all adverse mental states is one of the first essentials; the reason being that everything that is taking place in the human system is more or less affected by the states of mind. Anger wastes energy and invariably tends to produce a mean expression. But you will need all the energy you possess if you wish to remake yourself; and if you wish to produce in your personality a superior expression, all your expressions, even the slightest, must be of the very best. Worry dries up the cells and produces old-age conditions as well as those "dried up" conditions that are so detrimental to health, youth, vigor and personal charm. Every dried-up cell is a dead cell, and every dead cell adds so much more to personal weakness and personal inferiority. Fear retards natural and full expression; it also produces negative conditions and weakens the entire personality. No one can develop a strong, powerful, attractive personality until he has overcome fear, because every action of fear is an action of retreat; it moves to the rear; it gives up and drifts further and further back toward nothingness. The way to strength, power and higher development of every description, however, leads forward and forward continually. It is therefore most evident that no person can take the next step in human progress until anger, fear and worry have been removed from his life absolutely. But this is not impossible. Anger, fear and worry can be eliminated completely by anyone without any difficulty whatever.

Among other mental states that must be removed, we find grief, disappointment, discouragement, excitability, moroseness, the negative attitude, the critical attitude, the antagonistic attitude and states and attitudes of a similar nature. Cultivate the opposite states in every case, and the adverse ones will disappear. Live in perpetual sunshine; in fact, *be sunshine;* be the very spirit of joy, as there is nothing that is more conducive to the purpose you have in view than real, whole-hearted joy. Live in perpetual happiness, and inwardly feel the fullness of unbounded joy. And you can, when you learn to look at life from the proper point of view.

Another great essential is to love with every fiber of your being. The power of love is a great building power, provided it *is* love — the love that loves because it *is* love, and not because it wants something in return. Love that demands recompense or reward is not love; it is a misuse of the forces of mind, and therefore an obstacle in the way of greater things. Love with the love that *wants* to love; love all things with such a love, and with every fiber in your being; you thus, not only arouse the finest creative elements in your system, but you direct those elements to build in yourself the strong, the beautiful and the ideal.

The rebuilding of your personality must be carried out from within; the interior life must be reconstructed according to the ideal before the ideal can be made real in the external personality; and since the interior life is almost entirely controlled by the power of feeling, it is necessary that you train yourself to deeply feel every quality, condition or force that you wish to express. In the last analysis "you look the way you feel," and the way you feel depends upon what you imagine concerning yourself and what you habitually and subconsciously think about yourself. So long as you habitually and subconsciously feel ordinary, you will look ordinary; but as soon as you have trained your deeper feelings to feel the richness, the worth and the superiority of your true being, you will begin to express superiority and high worth in your personal appearance.

Continue to feel mean, ugly, miserable or disgusted, and you will finally look these things. Continue to feel disagreeable every hour for a year, or even less, and you will not only look disagreeable, but you will become personally repulsive. These are well-known facts; but the law works both ways. Continue to feel within yourself all those qualities that naturally attract admiration, and you will become so attractive, first in your nature and then also in your personality, that you will attract the admiration of every person you meet. Continue to feel any desirable quality, and that quality will become a living power in your nature. Later it will express itself in your personality, and you will look what you feel. This feeling, however, must be continuous; it must become habitual and subconscious, and must be thoroughly alive every hour.

Continue to feel life, power, purity, refinement, sweetness and loveliness, and these qualities will be expressed more and more in your personality. By feeling these things you cause them to become living forces in your interior life; and whatever is made alive and built up in the life within, will at once begin to work itself out and build itself into the external personality. You thus, through the elements of deep feeling, cause the ideal to actually become real; or, in other words, you cause the possibilities within to become living factors in the without.

To cultivate this high art of feeling in the within that you wish to express and build up in the without, *live* in the consciousness of the ideal and constantly *feel the fullness* of the ideal. When you feel the interior fullness of a quality you develop that quality, and the development will be similar in every respect to the ideal that animates what you feel. At first, special attention must be given to the *continuous feeling* of every quality that you wish to develop in your nature and in your personality; but gradually, as every feeling becomes subconscious, it will be second nature for you to feel the way you want to feel; *and when you feel the way you want to feel you will look the way you want to look.*

To apply the principle of feeling to the best advantage, the man should five in the consciousness of strength, power, capacity, quality and worth; and the woman should live in the consciousness of purity, refinement, beauty, loveliness and soul. Continue to feel *inwardly* the beautiful, and the beautiful will unfold itself in every atom in your being. Continue to feel the thrill of loveliness, fascination and personal charm in every fiber of your being, and you will not only become charmingly beautiful in personal appearance, but you will also gain that irresistible fascination that all the world admires so much in the truly developed feminine soul. Train yourself to feel refined, and you will express refinement in life, thought, speech, action and outward appearance. Train yourself to feel the sweetness of your ideal feminine nature, and you will become, in body, mind and soul, all that the term "human sweetness" can possibly imply.

Continue to inwardly feel strong and you develop a strong, attractive, masterful personality. Continue to feel in the within the fullness of strength and power, but do not permit this strong feeling to become overwrought or aroused beyond your absolute control. Be calm and poised while masterful and strong. Feel inwardly calm and inwardly strong, and you have the secret.

To continue to possess a personality that may rightly be termed an Edition de Luxe in human form, it is necessary to perfect such a personality more and more so long as we remain in personal existence. When we cease to promote progression we return to the ways of retrogression. An ideal personality can come only from an ideal life that is inwardly, actually and continually lived. When we cease to inwardly live the ideal and outwardly apply the ideal, our personal charms will begin to fade away. But those charms, when once gained, can be retained as long as we live, provided we continue to *live charmingly,* and continue to develop more and more every ideal quality that may exist in our nature.

You will never lose your strength or your power so long as you live to gain more and more strength and power. You will never lose your beauty, your loveliness or your sweetness so long as you live to become sweeter, more lovely and more beautiful than you ever were before.

The principles, methods and ideas presented in the preceding pages constitute the bridge, so to speak, over which we may pass into that new and vast domain where we may begin the next step in human progress; and having entered this domain, we are ready to take possession of the finer creative elements in the wonderful being of man, and direct those elements in such a manner as to produce any desired results in any special part of this new field. To begin, subjective concentration becomes the practical instrument through which these finer creative forces may be successfully applied; and we shall appreciate the great value of this instrument when we learn what can be accomplished through its scientific use.

Concentrate subjectively — *in deep feeling* — upon any part of the body, and you change the form of that part of the body to correspond with the ideal you clearly hold in mind during the concentration. This is a scientific fact, and one of the most important that this age has produced. You can prove it yourself. If there is a certain part of your face that you desire to have filled out, concentrate subjectively upon that part for a few minutes every hour, and in a few weeks you will note the desired change. You can do the same with any part of your body, because, through subjective concentration, you gain control of the finer creative elements of your system — those elements that are within and back of the cell structures, and that can produce any amount of new or improved cell structure as desired. Through subjective concentration you can not only modify the shape and the form of the body and build for yourself a more beautiful body, but you can also improve the quality of every fiber in your system; that is, you can increase or decrease the number of cells in any part and also change the fineness of those cells, just as the horticulturist develops a common-looking group of leaves into a most beautiful and highly cultivated flower.

Concentrate subjectively upon any quality in your nature, and you increase the power as well as the worth of that quality. And here we have a method through which any person can entirely change, for the better, his nature, his disposition, his character and his entire mentality. Concentrate subjectively upon any force in your system, and you not only increase the active power of that force, but you gain perfect control over the force itself, as well as its sphere of action. Concentrate subjectively upon any mental faculty or talent, and you awaken the real, interior power of that talent — that power that produces genius.

Concentrate subjectively upon any phase of consciousness, and you expand that consciousness continuously until you become conscious of worlds, realms and domains that you never dreamed of before. In brief, through subjective concentration, we may gain control of all the elements and forces that exist in the vastness of human life, and direct those elements in the re-making of ourselves according to our highest ideal. But this concentration is not the mere holding of attention here or there as we may elect. Subjective concentration is a special art — a very high art, and a most extensive art; it is the entering *into* the real essence of all substance and all force; it is the conveyance of a mental state or an ideal condition to any special part anywhere in the human system; it is *the living of the superior in that part where you wish the superior to be expressed.*

Steps to Higher Truths

When we proceed to consider what we know about the highest truth conceivable in our present state of development, we shall meet a very great paradox, and we shall also meet the reverse of this truth; that is, what we may term the only real sin possible to the human ego — the coming down from the perfect consciousness of this highest truth, which would constitute the great fall. And when we inquire to what this highest truth has reference, our answer must be that it is the truth concerning the most sublime principle of which we are conscious; and this can be nothing less than our own real or supreme self.

We understand that we may know many things concerning the external, but we may naturally know more about our own innermost nature than anything else that may have existence in the universe. Therefore, this highest truth necessarily declares something definite concerning our innermost or supreme self; and when this highest truth reveals itself we discover that the real or eternal self, that is, the soul or spirit of man, is now in possession of what we may term the All in All, and accordingly, has no needs or requirements whatever.

When we consider life in the external we find that existence has seemingly many needs and requirements; but we find that the spirit of man, the real eternal you, does not need anything whatever, being supplied abundantly with the All in All. Accordingly, the soul of man can, in justice and truth, ask for nothing, pray for nothing, desire nothing, hope for nothing, because the soul does have everything— "All that the Father hath is mine."

However we may consider the life of the individual, the needs of the personal man, or the requirements of the human phases of existence, we come invariably to the conclusion that everything that the personal or human side of life can possibly desire or require does, even now, exist in the human soul. The great kingdom has been given to man. The eternal I Am is in itself sufficient unto itself — having all life, all wisdom, all power, all joy, and is complete, perfect, and finished in the largest and highest significance of those terms.

When we consider this great truth, admittedly the highest truth that we can discern at the present time, we will, if our analysis be complete, meet the reverse; that is, the ignoring of this truth, which would involve the desire of the ego to seek for things in the external. And here is where we find the original sin, or the fall of man — going out or down into the external for anything whatever, when the soul or the spirit is already in possession of everything heart could wish for, or that the most perfect states of life might require.

Realizing the great truth that the human spirit, or the I Am, has everything needful for eternity, then we understand that if the Human Ego goes out into the external in search of pleasure, or wisdom, or power, or possessions, or help, or anything whatever, the Ego falls; and this is the only fall, the original fall, or the original sin of which we have heard so much during centuries past.

In the last analysis, there is only one sin possible to the Human Ego, and only one real mistake that the human entity can possibly make; and that sin is to leave the marvels and the riches of the spirit, wherein everything may be found — to leave the joys of the kingdom and the glories of the heaven within, and go out in search of lesser things.

Thus we must come inevitably to the conclusion that whenever we seek pleasure, or wisdom, or power directly and exclusively in or through external sources, we are committing again the original sin — we are repeating once more the great fall. And here is where we meet the great paradox; that is, what we should do with external things; if we should seek anything in the external; or try to enjoy any phase of existence that may appear on the outside of spiritual consciousness.

The great problem is this, if the soul in its glorified state always is in full possession of the Great Good, why should we seek anything whatever in the external. Why should we care for anything existing upon the outside. Indeed, could this be right under any circumstance. And how would it be possible to seek external joys, external wisdom and power, or anything that might seem of value in the external — how would it be possible to seek those things if the mere going out in search of them would constitute a sin or a fall? This is the great paradox, a seeming contradiction of the highest truth.

Turning our attention to an expression that reveals much light in this connection, we may quote a familiar statement, which declares, "Whenever you come to a place in supreme spiritual consciousness where you actually know that you are in need of nothing whatever, then you will find that everything in external life will begin to come into your world from every source conceivable."

There are a great many enlightened and powerful souls that have applied the principle of this law; and it proves itself invariably; but it is only the enlightened that can understand the reason why.

Considering another phase of the same idea, we realize that so long as we are going out, here and there, in search of what we need or desire, we are not true to ourselves; that is, we are not true to our highest and best self — that highest and best self that does possess everything we need. Briefly stated, we step down from our lofty position whenever we seek anything in the external; and accordingly, we become confused and lose our power. Therefore, whatever we may try to secure under such a circumstance, we shall fail, or at best we shall secure only fragments; and what comes into life through a mere attempt to search in the external for the needs of life will neither give real joy nor higher power.

This explains why the multitudes are never satisfied, because if they do not have what they want they are dissatisfied, and when they do receive what they thought they wanted, they are, in like manner, dissatisfied, because what they do receive under such a circumstance is but a fragment of the All in All. The soul, however, must be filled with the highest and best, and must be conscious of the All in All, if real joy is to obtain; and as the soul does possess inherently the All in All, being sufficient unto itself, we can readily imagine how we violate all the laws of life when we go out into the external in search of anything whatever.

Another great truth, or a vital phase of the same highest truth, is this, that so long as we retain our lofty position, realizing that we have everything, being all sufficient, having need of nothing from any source, and being so complete in ourselves, in our real supreme self, that we do not even need the universe, but could abide in serenity and perfection even though the universe should disappear — when we continue in that sublime realization, we establish ourselves in the very midst of the greatest power that the soul can possibly exercise. Indeed, at such a time consciousness Eves and moves and has its being in the very center of the Great Life, in the very light of the Great Wisdom and at the very heart of Limitless Power. Accordingly, the I Am, at such a time, is related perfectly to the Infinite, to the cosmos and to the entire world of things; that is, the I Am has its hold, so to speak, upon the entire situation, and can, not only master everything within its own world, but functions from that divine center of consciousness in supreme existence toward which the All-Good is moving eternally.

To state it differently, when you ascend to that supreme state of consciousness where you know that you have all things, including all power, you come into possession of the power to bring to yourself anything whatsoever, if you should so wish or desire.

When we appreciate this highest truth to the fullest degree, we shall indeed inquire again and again what we are to do with external things. But the problem is readily solved because the question is, not whether we are to ignore the external or to try to adapt ourselves to the external according to the light of this highest truth — these are not the questions involved; but the question is, whether we are to consider the external as of first importance, or look upon the manifested universe as something that is not absolutely necessary to our real existence, but that is a coming forth into external appearance of the All in All, the full possession of which we now have, and always will have for all eternity.

To use another expression, external things are not necessary to our happiness or wisdom or power any more than the rays from the sun are necessary to the existence of the sun; but because of the existence of the sun, the rays will continue to come forth perpetually; and in the same manner, because of the existence of the All in All in the soul and in the spiritual world, the manifestation of things will continue perpetually; and we can enjoy them as an expression, just as a genius enjoys his work, although knowing that his work is simply the result of what he is in himself, and of what he is doing with what he does possess within himself.

When we consider the element of happiness, which has been described as the highest good, we learn that we never find happiness if we go in search of happiness itself. True, we may find a few momentary pleasures through such a search; but those pleasures invariably produce undesirable reactions. The truth is, that we find happiness, not by seeking happiness directly, but by doing something that will result in happiness; and in all our doing, that is, if we wish to exercise our highest and greatest power in whatever we do, we must ascend to the consciousness of the Great Power existing in the soul. Therefore, by reasoning correctly, we understand that if we would live and work in the consciousness of the highest power of the soul, we would naturally produce those activities in consciousness that would result in the greatest happiness. In other words, the greatest happiness comes from the greatest work; and the greatest work is possible only in the consciousness of the greatest power — the power that we exercise and apply when we live and think in the realization of the great truth that the soul now is in possession of the All in All.

We may consider all forms of conditions and things, and we invariably find that they prove unsatisfactory so long as we go in search of them directly; that is, by seeking things in the external that we imagine may minister to our needs, we never find more than fragments; and the personal mind is half starved most of the time. However, when we remain in our lofty position, realizing that the soul is all-sufficient, having no need whatever — "All that the Father hath is mine" — then we discover that all kinds of desirable conditions, things, environments and situations begin to aggregate in our world — not because we need them absolutely, but because we invariably produce the aggregation of desirable conditions and things in the without whenever we begin to dwell in the consciousness of their spiritual correspondents within. In other words, while we are deeply conscious of the All in All within, we will attract the all-good from all sources in the without. Thus we explain the great mystery; that is, why the soul in its lofty position, where it feels that it has need of nothing, begins to draw towards itself everything.

To state the same truth in a different manner, we may emphasize the statement that when we enter that place in spiritual consciousness where we find everything, and where we find everything in its true and perfect position — when we live in that place we find that external conditions and things will begin to readjust themselves on every hand, working themselves out right, transforming themselves in every form and manner so as to harmonize, in their external state, with the perfect harmony and right position of what we have become conscious of, in that sublime state in the soul, where all is always well.

Here we discover how we create for ourselves a new heaven and a new earth, and how all things become new in the external when we have realized that which is forever new in the sublime within; that is, when we find the real heaven within, or become conscious of the newest and the highest states of being that we can realize in our present state of development, we observe that all external conditions will change to correspond; and thus we have a new earth — an external life as ideal and as perfect in the external as the new heaven is in the realms of interior consciousness. Furthermore, when we arise to this lofty state and assume our true position, which is to be conscious eternally of the supreme self, the Human Ego will again place itself in the midst of the Great Power — the Power that can do anything in the within or in the without — cause all things to rearrange themselves harmoniously, beautifully and perfectly to correspond with the perfect vision of the soul.

When we look upon the world in the without, we observe that vast multitudes are constantly looking in the external for what they think they need, never finding what satisfies, or coming in contact with what they describe as "the real thing." And the reason is, that the Human Ego in each one has stepped down, committed the original sin, searching in the without for that which we already possess in the within, and has repeated again and again the great fall. Thus every individual has, for the time being, lost the great power, come down from the lofty position of spiritual consciousness, and is to that degree out of place, out of tune and out of harmony, more or less, with everything and everybody. Thus multitudes go through the world dissatisfied and heart hungry — miserable creatures physically and mentally, never finding exactly what they desire, and always dreaming of some future time when all needs shall be supplied and all wrongs shall be righted.

This is the condition of vast multitudes; but how readily they could change their condition — how soon they could absolutely transform their personal life and their entire world of manifestation, changing everything, causing everything to become as they wish it to be; for indeed, the very moment they would arise and re-establish themselves in their true position, in the full consciousness of this highest truth, they would know that we have the All in All now — that the All in All does exist in the spiritual life of every individual this moment and forever; and that we all may live in the spiritual, should continually live in the spiritual, upon the heights of supreme consciousness, in the realization of the limitlessness inheritance of the Supreme Self.

When we understand these things we realize the uselessness of working so hard to change conditions and environments in the external, as many do, literally working the body to death in order to produce certain external conditions that we imagine to be desirable — wearing life away in producing conditions which in the end prove themselves to be entirely inadequate to the real needs of the real man. We understand clearly how useless it is to pursue such a course when the eternal I Am, the spirit of man, already is in possession of the All in All, being sufficient unto itself, having its true being in that lofty state where the soul has received the kingdom — where we fully realize the largest and highest significance of the great statement, "All that the Father hath is mine."

When we proceed to apply in practical life the principle of this highest truth, we may in the beginning inquire whether or not we can accept that principle in full, when we see on every hand in the visible world the lack of things needful, as well as any number of unrealized ideals; and the answer is, that so long as we continue to live down among things, expecting to secure what we desire through the search of things, we shall not be able to appreciate the real meaning of this highest truth. But the moment we arise to that lofty position of the spirit wherein we know "what God has prepared for them that love Him," we find ourselves in the very midst of the great fight of this truth, and in consequence we can say, in all conviction and sincerity, "I have everything."

Whenever we have made efforts in the past to cause consciousness to transcend the temporal and enter into the light of the spiritual, we have met with experiences of a very striking nature; that is, so long as we lived down in the temporal, or in that state of material consciousness that has been described as "this world," we were constantly confronted with what we might term the awfulness of adversity, trouble and wrong; and upon many instances seemed so engulfed in confusion that we did not know where to turn; and all of those distressing conditions seemed, not only very real, but seemed to combine sufficient power to overcome us completely. However, when we began to look up towards the lofty places, and began to lift the mind, causing consciousness to rise more and more until we found ourselves upon the heights of the spiritual — when we found ourselves in that position, we realized that adversity had become so insignificant as to mean practically nothing. Trouble and sorrow had vanished into the distance and was scarcely discernible any more, while confusion and darkness had completely disappeared beneath the glory and the light in which we now were living, moving and having our being.

We all have had experiences of this kind, illustrating how real adversity and confusion seems to be while we are down among things; and how insignificant trouble, evil and wrong become when we permit the soul to take wings and ascend to the loftier heights. In other words, while we are down among things, we do not seem to have anything that is satisfactory, and mostly everything seems to be against us; but when we transcend "this world" and enter the light of the spirit, then everything changes. We find ourselves in possession of everything that we wanted — we are conscious of the fullness of the all-good; and instead of conditions being against us, everything is for us, coming more and more into our world, bringing from every source the spirit and truth of the heart's desire.

Considering this experience we may justly inquire as to its real significance, whether or not it is a demonstration of the law, or merely a seeming change for the better due to a change of attitude; and it may seem to be the latter at times; that is, we may enter into a state of mind wherein everything seems better, although in the world of hard cold facts there may be no change whatever; and this may be true at times and for a period; but we all shall discover most positively that even the hard cold facts of the practical world will respond and change absolutely provided we continue to five upon the spiritual heights, and continue to affirm this highest truth *that we have everything now* — that we have the all in all, being sufficient unto ourselves, created as we are in the image of the Supreme, and having in our possession the riches of the Infinite.

We shall find, through actual demonstration, that so long as we maintain our lofty position in the spiritual consciousness of this highest truth, never under any circumstance coming down, or giving way to any seeming contradiction of this truth — so long as we continue in that lofty position, we will gradually and surely cause everything, both in the without and in the within, to change more and more until our entire world, visible and invisible, tangible and intangible, has become exactly similar to our own sublime realization of truth.

Approaching again the great paradox — when you realize in spiritual consciousness that you have everything, and therefore need not go in search of anything, it is then that everything that you have ever desired, or wished for, or asked for, will come to you in boundless supply from every source — when we consider this paradox from other viewpoints, we may well ask ourselves, "Why should it be necessary for everything to come to us that we might have desired in the past when we have become conscious of that sublime state of being where we feel that we are not in need of anything?" This, however, is something that we can understand only as we become spiritually conscious, and discern clearly the true relationship between that which remains forever in the absolute, and that which is forever coming forth into manifestation.

In reality the soul or the spirit is not in need of things; and therefore if we wish to Eve in perfect harmony with the life of the soul, we must not think it necessary to go in search of things in order to secure pleasure, wisdom or power. But aside from this great truth, the soul, when living its full life, will give expression to its own joy, to its own wisdom, to its own power; and all such expressions will find manifestation through those external things that correspond to the life and the ideals of the soul.

Again, the soul is sufficient unto itself in every form and manner; and yet it is not the purpose of the soul simply to live merely in the consciousness of that state of all-sufficiency. It is also the purpose of the soul to bring forth, in ever-increasing measure, the elements and qualities of that state of all-sufficiency; and this bringing forth will cause life in the personality to be related to the world of things, and related harmoniously in proportion to the perfection of our consciousness of this all-sufficiency of the soul.

To state it differently, if we are only partially conscious of the all-sufficiency of the soul, we will be harmoniously related to the world of things only in isolated places, while more or less at variance with the larger part of the visible world; but as we grow in the consciousness of this all-sufficiency of the soul, we will manifest more and more of the life and wisdom and power of the soul, and thereby cause a larger measure of the world of things to be related harmoniously to our own personal existence. To use a kindred expression, the more of the harmony of the soul we become conscious of, the more harmony we will establish in our own world of things; and also the more of the fullness of the life bf the soul we become conscious of, the more of the good and the true and the perfect will we realize in the outer world of things, proving the law that external things, as they exist or act in our personal world, will correspond exactly with our state of consciousness in the within.

It may require much deep thought to discern the significance of this analysis; but if we look upon external things as merely channels for expression, and never think of things as absolute necessities to the real life of the soul, we will understand more perfectly the meaning of this highest truth. To use a simple illustration: We cannot find real pleasure among things provided we seek such pleasure among things exclusively, being at the time unconscious of the real joy of the soul; but when we become conscious of the real joy of the soul, and proceed to express that joy *through* external things, it is then that things serve their true purpose, adding thereby to the joy of the soul; because here it is most important to understand that the inner consciousness of the higher joy of the soul increases in proportion to the measure of that joy we express.

We can find an illustration of this truth in the world of music; that is, however great the joy and the privilege of the musical genius may be in the mere fact that he is conscious of his power to give music, his joy and privilege will increase remarkably the moment he proceeds to express that music through a perfect instrument. In like manner, the joy of the soul, in its own sublime consciousness of the all-joy, may be marvelous beyond words; nevertheless, when the soul begins to express that joy in the world of things, immediately the *feeling* of joy in the within will increase accordingly.

Thus we understand that, although the world of things is not necessary to the full life of the soul as lived in the spirit, nevertheless, the life of the soul becomes infinitely more wonderful and enjoyable as it is given expression in the outer world; and that is why we have the manifested universe with its innumerable spheres, visible and invisible.

The same truth, if applied in another direction, would lead us to the conclusion that all the souls in the cosmos, frequently described as "the great white throng," are as necessary to God as God is necessary to that innumerable host; and to express this idea briefly, we would simply say that, although the Infinite is sufficient in the fullest and highest significance of that term, nevertheless, the expression of Divine Life, individualized in countless millions of human entities, is a privilege far beyond the power of any mind to conceive; because the joy of Infinite Life increases in proportion to the measure of expression of that life in the consciousness of human souls who have the power to partake and manifest that joy. If we are spiritually conscious we can discern this very clearly; and it is a truth that is wonderfully rich with spiritual wisdom — a truth which when discerned will change remarkably our understanding of the Supreme. Furthermore, when we know that we exist as spiritual entities, not in some vague, indefinable realm only, but because we are necessary to the greatest joy and privilege of the Supreme — that we are necessary in this manner throughout eternity— when we realize this great truth, we shall indeed pause to think as we never thought before.

Returning to that phase of the subject that we shall have to consider in living up to this highest truth, we must constantly bear in mind the principle that we must become conscious of the allness of life and power in the within before we can demonstrate the power to cause all things desired to come to us in the without; and when we realize further that things have no value in themselves, but become valuable only as channels for expression, we understand how absolutely necessary it is to continue in that lofty position where we are fully conscious of the possession of everything that can possibly exist in the life of the soul. But as the soul lives perpetually in a desire to express its all-sufficiency — it is when we become deeply conscious of that desire that we can really appreciate the true purpose of things; and it is then that we make a most important discovery concerning the true relationship between the spirit of things and things themselves. And through this discovery we find that we do not secure power from things; but we can, when we live in the spirit, give power to things — give power to everything, and thereby manifest our own power in the external in perfect accord with our consciousness of that power in the within. And again, we must remember that however great our joy our wisdom or power may be in the perfect consciousness of the soul, that joy wisdom and power will consciously increase through expression.

In this connection we might with much interest consider another phase of the same principle; that is, that the privilege of being alive, although very great, is not nearly as great as the privilege of *living* life; and the reason is, that when we are simply alive we are conscious of life only in its passive or inactive state; but when we begin to *live* life, then we cause life to go forth in a thousand different directions; and accordingly, life becomes a thousand times more interesting. This fact, if considered in connection with all other modes of expression, will give emphasis to the statement made, that the soul although all-sufficient in itself, finds far greater joy in its all-sufficiency when that all-sufficiency begins to manifest throughout the visible and tangible world of things.

To consider this idea in a very practical manner, we will turn our attention to the fact that nearly every mind of ambition is constantly in search of external advantages or more worthy opportunities. Accordingly, we find all such minds going out in search of greater opportunities, or in search of external channels for more worthy or more wonderful accomplishments; and in a measure these things are found; but only in a measure, and for the time being — no permanent satisfaction ever arising from such a mode of procedure. However, if these minds would first search for the greater power within, that is, the all-sufficiency of power, realizing that every advantage, opportunity or privilege exists potentially in the life of the soul even now — if the mind would first enter into that extraordinary realization, the power desired would at once arise in consciousness; that is, that power within through which every individual can create his own opportunities, his own privileges and his own channels of richer expression. Thus, instead of going out into the external in search of something that will have to be created from the within before it can possibly exist in the external — instead of taking that round-about way, usually finding nothing, we may, by entering directly into the consciousness of the all-sufficiency of the soul, secure the very power through which we can create for ourselves any external opportunity, privilege or advantage that we may wish to apply in connection with any object or ambition we have in mind.

When we understand these things we realize that there is no contradiction in the statement that, having everything already we should not go in search of anything. But there is a seeming contradiction so long as we view this highest truth from the consciousness of the personal only. The fact is, we should not go in search of things for the mere sake of possessing things, or in the mistaken belief that we can find in things what we need or desire. We should take another course entirely, and first seek the consciousness of that higher power within that can, when manifested in the without, *do anything desired with things* — a power that can create any condition among things, or attract any combination of things or quality of elements or forces whatever according to the object we have in view.

To use a familiar statement, we can do anything desired with effects when we gain the power to master completely the original cause of all such effects. But that power we cannot gain so long as we live down in the world of things, believing that we are subject to things or dependent upon things, or that we can secure happiness, wisdom, power or a richer life through a certain peculiar combination of things. Such a belief is the very reverse of the highest truth, which declares, that we are not directly dependent upon anything in the external, because we have, not only the all in all in spiritual consciousness, but through the possession of the all in all we have that power that can, when applied externally, do everything conceivable with the external world.

Another important statement to hold constantly before mind is this, that we secure a certain desirable combination of things in the without only as we gain the consciousness of the ideal of that combination in the higher life of the real and the true. But we cannot become conscious of that ideal excepting in this sublime state where we know that we have everything.

When we consider the needs of the personal life, as found among those who live exclusively in the world of things, we discern on every hand persons that feel as if they could not exist another day unless they secured certain conditions, certain privileges or certain tangible things that seem absolutely necessary. And they live constantly in that attitude, receiving temporary satisfaction upon occasions, but never securing what they think they positively must have in order to live. And the reason is, that they are looking in the world of effect for that which cannot appear in the world of effect until it has been created by the natural cause in the within.

We may grope in darkness for ages, thinking we cannot exist another moment until we receive the light, and yet so long as we continue to grope in darkness, never thinking of how we might *produce* the light, we will continue in the blackness of the darkness without change. But the very moment we go to the source of light, and give attention to that source, we produce the light, and the awful darkness disappears completely.

However, the great source of everything that we may desire or need can be found only in that sublime state of consciousness wherein we know that the soul is in possession of the all-sufficiency — in need of nothing, having within itself the limitless life, wisdom, power and riches of the Infinite. It is then that we can give real action to the sublime source of the Great Light; and when we do give such action, the Great Light will go forth throughout the entire world of consciousness. And what we become conscious of, that we shall invariably bring forth in the visible world.

When we understand this highest truth, we discover for the first time the meaning of that wonderful statement, "Be true to yourself," because it is only as you take this lofty position where you realize that you are *the true self,* that you become conscious of the all-sufficiency of the soul; in other words, we can be true to the self only when we know what the self really is, and what the self really can do. But on the contrary, we cannot be true to the self so long as we go in search among things for those needs of life that the self alone can provide. This is what it means "to grieve the spirit away"; to deny Higher Power, believing that we can find what we want in "this world." However, when we arrive to that higher consciousness where we realize that the all in all is in the spirit only, in the spiritual life of the supreme self, then we no longer deny the Holy Spirit, nor the Christ, nor the Infinite. We rely upon the whole truth, the highest truth; and we receive that greater power that invariably appears in consciousness when we discern this highest truth.

To state it differently, when we find our true position in life — and we find our true position only as we establish ourselves in our loftiest position — when we begin to live in that lofty position, which is the true position, we understand that it is then and then only that we can five life as life should be lived, and relate ourselves to things in such a way as to use all things according to the law of manifestation and the law of growth and advancement in personal life; that is, it is only after we have taken our true place in life and consciousness that we can do anything right. And when we begin to do everything right, then we can readily understand what a marvelous change must come over our entire world.

The more we think of this highest truth the more clearly we appreciate its real significance; but while we are on the way to the full understanding of this highest truth it is well to consider the immediate value of accepting this truth, even though its greatest power has not as yet become manifested. To illustrate: When we accept the idea that the human soul, being in possession of everything necessary to life, and when we realize that the spirit of man can, therefore, need nothing, or lose nothing — when this startling truth is realized, we shall never be depressed, dissatisfied or disappointed with external conditions, no matter how disappointing those conditions may for the time being seem to be.

When we take that lofty position, realizing that we have it all, and therefore, we can in reality experience neither loss, grief nor disappointment — when we take that higher ground, what an immense change we will produce, not only in our own attitude towards life, but in our own state of mind, in our own feelings, desires and mental actions; in fact, our mode of thought and action will change absolutely; and instead of grieving when conditions seem to be adverse, we will continue in the consciousness of the great truth that we have everything and that all is well.

In the beginning, the practical value of such an attitude will simply be to give us sublime peace of mind no matter what may transpire; but the taking of that higher ground will work wonders in the course of time, because if we continue to live in the conviction that we have it all, and that all is well, we will continue to create the perfect and the ideal in our own consciousness, creating the perfect and the ideal more wonderfully, and upon a grander scale every day; and according to the great law, whatever we create in consciousness we will invariably experience, attract, produce and possess in the external in due time. In consequence, we do not simply give the mind peace by living in the conviction that the soul is all-sufficient now, in need of nothing, beyond all loss, grief or disappointment. We accomplish infinitely more than merely this peace of mind, because, while living in that lofty position, we continue to *live* the highest truth — to express and manifest the life, the wisdom, the light and the power of the highest truth. And in due time, such expression will appear in the visible and in the tangible, which will mean the transformation of the external according to the image and likeness of the highest truth — the consciousness of which we have lived so faithfully and so well.

Thus we realize that whatever the person may think or feel, or however conditions may appear in the external, we have everything to gain by taking this higher ground now; and we all can. Then as we proceed, we will demonstrate more and more that the law is absolutely true; we shall not have to live very long in that lofty place, in the consciousness of the power of the spirit, until that power will begin to make changes for the better in mind and body and in external conditions. Furthermore, we will demonstrate continuously the power of that great statement, "When one is lifted up, hundreds and thousands will be lifted up." When we take this great step, we will become instrumental in leading, first, a few to do the same, then a larger number, until later we may inspire a vast throng to take the same higher ground, the final results of which will be marvelous beyond words to describe.

We know that the greatest movements in the world have originated in this manner — some great soul taking higher ground, and a few coming up to the same lofty place later; and gradually a larger number began to apply the same idea until the movement itself became an inspiration to the race. We can do this very thing now upon a larger scale than anything ever attempted in the past, because we are not dealing simply with the light of some valued idea — we are dealing with nothing less than the light of the highest truth; and therefore, the possibilities of a spiritual movement having for its purpose the living up to this highest truth — the possibilities of such a movement are so numerous and so wonderful that we shall, in order to appreciate the outcome, cause our imagination to extend its power into the highest and largest realms conceivable; and even then, we shall be able to imagine only a part of what we may accomplish in taking such a course — proceeding now regardless of time, circumstance or condition to live up to this highest truth — to *know* that we have everything that heart can desire — living in the very life of the Supreme.

Steps to the Spiritual

The first essential in giving scientific attention to the study of the spiritual world is to realize that, what we speak of as the spiritual world, is not necessarily synonymous with the invisible world. And here we find one of the chief obstacles to spiritual advancement; that is, that we have, in too many instances, made the terms "spiritual" and "invisible" synonymous, and accordingly have come to the conclusion that an experience in the invisible is also a spiritual experience, or that a gain made in our understanding of the invisible would also imply a gain in our understanding of the spiritual.

The fact is, however, that these two terms are not synonymous — the invisible does not necessarily contain any more of the spiritual than does the visible; but wherever we do proceed in the belief that the invisible is synonymous with the spiritual, we are very liable to turn our attention away from the spiritual, instead of entering into higher realizations of the spiritual.

We must begin this study by understanding, in the first place, that the invisible world, so-called, is only an extension of the visible world; and therefore, what we speak of as the invisible universe is simply elements and forces found in the physical universe manifesting in higher grades of vibration.

As an illustration, we may take the force of fight, which manifests in the visible through certain grades of vibration, but manifests also in a number of higher grades of vibration, spoken of as the higher octaves of light; but the only difference between visible light and the higher octave's of light is this, that the vibrations in the latter are more rapid than in the former. Therefore, we cannot speak of the invisible rays of light as spiritual, any more than we can speak of the visible rays of light as spiritual. The only difference between the visible and the invisible is a matter of speed in the vibrations.

We are surrounded with elements on every hand that are purely physical, and yet not visible to physical sense — the atmosphere, as an illustration; but we have learned, through experiments, that there are also finer grades of atmosphere so delicate and so high in the scale of vibration that they cannot be discerned through any of our physical senses. However, those finer grades of atmosphere are not necessarily spiritual simply because they are beyond the discernment of physical sense.

We might analyze the entire tangible universe in the same manner, and we would find, in each instance, that forces and elements manifesting in the physical universe may and do manifest through higher and finer grades of expression, as high in the scale as we may wish to go; but in no instance are these so-called higher expressions of force or substance any more spiritual than those expressions of force and substance that we can feel, weigh and measure upon the physical plane.

The reason for this is found in the fact that spirituality is something entirely different from the mere manifestation of life, force, substance or power upon any plane, no matter how high, delicate or wonderful that plane may be.

We may illustrate the same principle by comparing two human beings, one very crude in expression and appearance, while the other very refined and highly developed, so far as mind and personality are concerned; but this would not prove that the refined personality would necessarily be more spiritual than the crude personality, although if the individual of refinement should undertake the development of spirituality, he would advance far more rapidly towards the spiritual heights than the individual who was still lacking in refinement of personality, thought and mind.

You may examine two distinct forms of intellect in the same manner, one developed to a very high degree, as far as intellect is concerned, while the other decidedly undeveloped in the intellectual world; but again the intellect with high development would not necessarily appreciate the spiritual, nor even the moral any better than the intellect that was lacking in purely intellectual development. But the same would be true as in the former illustration, with regard to possibility of spiritual development; that is, the finer the intellect the more rapidly can the mind develop along all lines, even spiritual lines, provided such development is undertaken.

We know, however, that a great many highly intellectual people are absolutely lacking in spiritual appreciation and cosmic consciousness; although their minds are wonderful in the intellectual world, still they are practically blind when it comes to things spiritual.

Then on the other hand, we find a great many people who are not developed intellectually, but who may have a certain degree of appreciation of the spiritual. This does not prove, however, that intellect is an obstacle to spiritual development. On the contrary, it is a most important essential, provided we undertake spiritual development in earnest. But, knowing all these things, we realize that intellect itself, no matter how refined or how wonderful it may be, does not, in itself, constitute spirituality.

The truth is, that an individual may be wonderfully developed in personality, in mind, in talent, in genius and in all the higher and finer elements and qualities of life, and yet be totally unconscious of the spiritual side of life.

In like manner, an individual may be highly developed in the so-called psychic world and be practically master of all the phases of the sixth sense, thereby having the power to look into the invisible world as if it were an open book, and yet be totally unconscious of the spiritual world and without the least spiritual development.

All these facts prove that what we speak of as the higher, or the finer or the invisible, does not produce or constitute spirituality. The truth is, we may rise to the very highest states of attainment in the so-called invisible universe, without taking a single step in advance into the spiritual world. And the reason why we understand when we realize that spirituality is something entirely different from anything that appears anywhere in the manifested universe, no matter how high in manifestation the appearance may come forth.

Regardless of our development along any line, we must add something entirely different if we wish spirituality, or if we desire to enter into the spiritual world.

In many instances, that something else appears in minds that are neither refined nor developed; but minds that are lacking in refinement and development cannot go very far into the spiritual; so that we shall find it an advantage to further our own development along all fines when we have higher spiritual attainments in view.

We may know something about the spiritual without having gone very far in the development of mind, personality, life or character; but the farther we go in the development of personality, life, mind and character, the higher we may go in spiritual development, provided we find the key to the spiritual world.

But we must, under every circumstance, have that key; because if we do not have the key to the spiritual world, we shall not find spirituality, no matter how wonderfully we may be developed along all other lines, including the understanding of the invisible universe.

On every hand we find people who have undertaken the study of the invisible, thinking that they may, through that source, gain absolute knowledge of life, and in that manner find the real solution for all the problems of life. But here we must remember again that the so-called invisible universe does not contain the secret, because the invisible, as well as the visible, is merely an effect. The cause of all manifestation is found only in the great within of the spiritual world. You will not get any nearer to the real principle of life or wisdom by furthering your study of the so-called invisible forces and elements of life, nor will you become more deeply conscious of the presence of the Infinite through development along these invisible lines.

The reason is, that in any case, you will be dealing simply with manifestation; and you will not enter into that marvelous something that exists back of manifestation until you enter into the real consciousness of the spiritual world.

The power of the spirit can be found only in the spiritual world, and may not be found in matter or force, no matter how high in the scale of the invisible world matter or substance or force may manifest.

To find the spirit of things, we must enter into the spirit of things; and we enter into the spirit of things only when we become conscious of the spiritual world — that world of reality and principle and life that has its being within the entire cosmos, but that does not appear in differentiated form anywhere in the world of manifestation.

We also realize that we can understand cause only by entering into the consciousness of cause; but here we should remember that cause does not exist in the invisible any more than in the visible. On the contrary, cause exists back of the invisible as well as back of the visible, these two being, under every circumstance, merely effects of the Real Cause of everything, which may be found only in the spiritual world.

It is clearly evident, therefore, that we cannot understand the spiritual world merely through a study of the invisible. We must turn our attention in another direction; and when we do, we shall find that there is just as much spirit in the within of visible substance as there is in the within of invisible substance; and also, we shall find the power of the spirit expressing itself just as fully in visible force as it does in invisible force, although a greater measure of this power may sometimes be found expressing itself in the higher grades of invisible life, the difference there would be, not in kind, but in quantity.

When we consider the subject from this true understanding of life, we will naturally inquire what we really do know about the spiritual world. It is quite true that we know a great deal about the invisible world. Modern science is making it possible for an individual to gain direct information concerning what we have spoken of as things invisible. We may, through certain instruments, discern higher octaves of light, such as the X-Rays and the N-Rays— forces of light that cannot be discerned through the physical eye unaided. We are also able to measure higher vibrations of sound that cannot be heard by the physical ear unaided. In like manner, we are able to detect substances and elements higher up in the scale of manifestation — elements that appear intangible to physical sense, and yet prove themselves, through experiments, to be just as tangible as the solid rock with which we all are familiar.

We are exploring the unknown in every realm of the invisible universe, and we are finding facts and information of inestimable value; but this information gives us absolutely nothing about the spiritual world, the reason for which our preceding analysis has demonstrated conclusively.

A scientist may be able to use the X-Ray and the N-Ray, and any number of higher and finer rays of light, understanding them perfectly, comprehending the laws through which they manifest, but this power does not make him spiritual.

An occult scientist may be able to discern some of the finest forces in the invisible world, and may be able to detect, through the sixth sense, all kinds of manifestations and modes of life upon higher planes; but this does not make him spiritual, or give him the least added insight into the spiritual world.

In many instances, this so-called higher knowledge of invisible things will, for a time, become an obstacle to real spiritual understanding, because the individual may imagine for a time that he has found, through his knowledge of the invisible, the real secret of spiritual things.

The same may be true of the physical scientist. He may become so enthused over his ability to penetrate the unknown with his wonderful instruments that he may imagine for a time that the unknown is nothing more than an extension of the known, and that it is all force and matter after all, appearing in different grades of vibration. He defines the invisible, or the unknown, as simply more rapid vibrations of force and matter; but, to his mind, it is all force and matter; and in consequence, he remains, in his conception of things, as materialistic as he was before.

We realize that knowledge along all lines will, in the long run, prove advantageous, both in our ability to master the visible and the invisible, and in our ability to discern the spiritual. But, as stated previously, we must find the key to the spiritual world before we can enter that world; that key, however, cannot be found simply through a knowledge of visible or invisible elements or forces. We must search in an entirely different direction.

The first essential will be to realize clearly and absolutely that the spiritual world and the invisible world are not the same. The second essential will be to realize that we cannot find the spiritual world by going up in the scale of vibration of manifested expression; but that we can find the spiritual world only by entering into the *spirit* of the unmanifested within that exists back of all manifestations; or in other words, that has its being in the Changeless Soul of the universe. When we enter the spirit of all life, we find a state wherein all being is as it is for all time; and in that state we find the All in All — a state to which nothing can be added and nothing taken away.

When we examine the various visible or invisible states of life, however, we invariably find conditions to which something can be added, or from which something can be taken away. And herein we shall find the real secret to the spiritual life, or to the spiritual state of being; that is, whenever you discern a state of being to which nothing can be added, or nothing taken away, then you may know that you are conscious of the spirit, or that you have entered into the spiritual world.

On the other hand, whenever you meet a state of existence wherein you find that something might be added, or taken away, you are not dealing with the real spiritual world, but with the manifested world, the world of change and growth and development, existing as it does, not only upon the visible plane, but upon millions and millions of invisible planes, ascending higher and higher in the scale of ever advancing manifestation.

When we enter the spiritual world we find real being itself; but real being is something that cannot be defined in words. It is something that we must become conscious of individually; and we do become conscious of real being when we experience that consciousness of being that reveals to us unmistakably the great truth that to this being nothing can be added or taken away.

When we analyze the great universe of manifestation, visible and invisible, we find that it is eternally becoming; it is incomplete everywhere, and subject to development along all lines for eternity. But this is not true of the spiritual world. The spiritual world is finished even now; it is complete in the absolute sense, containing within itself the All in All; and when we actually enter into the spiritual world, and become conscious of the All in All, we shall know for ourselves that within the spiritual world nothing can be added or taken away. Thus we may declare with the illumined Mind of other days, "It is finished, and it is all very good."

When we approach the study of the spiritual we must invariably bear in mind the truth that everything existing in, or pertaining to, the spiritual is in itself complete; and also that our mental attitude, when undertaking such study, must proceed in the conscious recognition of this great truth — recognizing definitely and continually the principle of absolute perfection and completeness in everything that involves the elements of the spiritual.

In approaching the study of the soul we must employ the same method, because the soul is absolutely spiritual, and therefore contains within itself everything that is necessary to the life and eternal existence of the soul. We know that mind and body are incomplete, which is true of everything finding expression in the external; that is, wherever we find expression, there we shall find completeness, because expression is at best only a partial coming forth of the limitless that exists in the spiritual within.

This being true, we realize that development and advancement would involve the continual increase of expression in every form and manner — an increase that is necessarily perpetual, because there can be no end to the increase of that which is, in reality, limitless.

When we proceed with the analysis of anything in life, we meet the same principles and conditions; that is, we find incompleteness in the external no matter how high in the scale the external may manifest; and we meet absolute completeness in the within of everything, whether it be a quality, a principle, an entity or a universe. The spiritual within of everything is complete and changeless, and that is the reason why it is spiritual.

To consider the more practical side of the subject, we may examine the principle of health and wholeness; and we shall discover the existence of a principle of health having its being within the life of all kinds of health, and that this principle contains every element of health that is conceivable or possible. In other words, the principle of perfect health contains so much health that it would be impossible to contain any more; and therefore the real principle of health is purely spiritual, containing within itself an unlimited measure of real or absolute health.

This being true, we realize the necessity of going to the inner or spiritual source for health, wholeness, life, vitality, power, if we would secure the largest possible measure and the finest and most perfect conceivable quality.

We may examine any quality in the same manner, or any state of the mind, or of consciousness; and we shall find that even though the external expression may be incomplete, the inner source is absolutely complete, so that the without can continue to draw upon the within for an endless period of time, constantly receiving more without at any time exhausting the source of supply.

This being true, we realize that no matter how much we may possess of the richness or perfection of life, either in personality, in mind or in soul, we can always receive more from the spiritual within, and continue to receive more without any end — rising thereby in the scale along all lines perpetually. However, we must, before we can apply this wonderful law, understand perfectly the great truth that the spiritual is perfect, complete and inexhaustible, and that the spiritual is the real, immeasurable source of everything that appears in the outer world.

When we consider individuals in the light of this idea and speak of them as spiritual, we cannot possibly mean that they are spiritual through and through, or in the absolute sense, but that they are growing in the consciousness of the spiritual, and thereby drawing more and more upon the perfection of the soul for external expression in mind and personality.

The outer life is always incomplete, always growing, always developing, always advancing, while the inner life is constantly giving forth more and more from its inexhaustible perfection for the purpose of increasing the perfection, the richness and the worth of external life; and any individual who is constantly bringing forth from the spiritual within more and more of the richness, the quality and the life of the spirit, is constantly becoming more spiritual in consciousness and in realization; and therefore we can speak of such an individual as being upon the great spiritual path.

An individual, however, who has not become conscious of the spiritual within, and is accordingly depending exclusively upon the limitations of the outer life, has not as yet entered upon the spiritual path, and therefore reveals in personality, in mind and in thought only those elements that pertain to personal life, or the earth, earthy.

But we all are destined in due time, to become conscious of the spirit, and thereby begin the expression of the spiritual through every phase of external life; but as this is an endless process, no individual soul will, at any time, come to a place where the full expression of the spirit will become tangible in external life; and this is well, because if we should reach such a state, then life would come to a standstill, and there would be nothing further to live for in the future.

When we realize the full significance of life and its development, we find that we live in two worlds, or that we all should live in two worlds if we would be true to the great purpose that existence has in view. These two worlds constitute the great within and the great without, or the spiritual within which is inexhaustible perfection, and the external without which is eternally receiving a greater and a greater degree of expression from the spiritual, and thereby ever becoming more wonderful, more beautiful and more ideal.

The majority, however, live almost entirely in the without, and only upon rare occasions come into conscious contact with the spiritual within. That is the principal reason why the majority is materialistic and five in bondage to illness, adversity and pain, meeting the wrong on every hand and gaining only fragments of that which is conducive to goodness and joy.

To live in such a state of mind, however, is to depend almost exclusively upon the limitations of the without, and therefore such an existence will not mean very much under any circumstance. But when we proceed to live as much in the spiritual within as we do in the tangible without, we shall find that every moment will become larger, more wonderful and more desirable, because we are constantly drawing upon the richness of the spiritual for perpetual increase in the external; and we know that there can be no greater joy than the consciousness of continuous ascension into the larger, the richer and the higher in life, thought and sublime realization.

To make practical application of this mode of living, we should enter as frequently as possible, and as deeply as possible, into the consciousness of the purely spiritual — into the realization of that world wherein all things are absolutely perfect and inexhaustible, so that we may receive an ever-increasing measure, not only of life, but of all the elements and qualities of life, thereby increasing constantly the value, the worth, the meaning and the power of personal existence; that is, we should be conscious of the spirit continually, and should continually aim to build up, refine, develop and perfect everything in mind and personality. But in order that we may proceed in the application of this principle, we must live in two worlds at a time; we must live in the tangible without and also in the spiritual within.

When we appreciate the real significance of the spiritual world, and know that it is a world permeating all other worlds in the vastness of the cosmos, and that this spiritual world is so constituted that it contains within itself everything that eternity may require for life, advancement and ascension, we will naturally inquire how we may know more about the spiritual, and also examine our minds with a view of ascertaining how much we know about the spiritual at the present time.

When these questions have been answered, we will ask ourselves how we learned what we know about the spiritual, or how we became conscious of those spiritual elements that we know we are conscious of in our present stage of realization. When we know these things we shall be better able to proceed further, and therefore such questions are most important.

When we attempt to define the spiritual we begin by declaring that the spiritual world is absolute; and we know that that which is absolute is in a state wherein nothing can be added; but we do not find it possible to conceive of such a state so long as our consciousness is purely personal. The appreciation of the spiritual, therefore, is something that cannot be gained until we first develop at least a measure of spiritual discernment; but we all do possess a certain measure of spiritual discernment, and therefore we have a foundation upon which to build the great structure of limitless spiritual consciousness.

We speak of the Divine as absolute because we realize that we can add nothing to the wisdom, the power, the life, the light and the glory of the Supreme. We say that God is All in All, but we can say the same of the spiritual world.

When we examine the external world, however, we find the very reverse. We may ascend continually in the scale of development until we become marvels, far beyond the power of imagination to picture, and yet we can still go higher. We can still attain greater power, greater wisdom, greater attainments. The same is true of everything that exists in the great without. No matter how wonderful it may be, we can still make it more wonderful, and we can continue to make it more and more wonderful during the innumerable aeons of eternity.

Thus we appreciate the fact that that which manifests in the great without, no matter how marvelous or how high in the scale it may be, whether it exists in the visible or in the very highest phases of the invisible, it is nevertheless external — you can always add something more, you can always make it more perfect or more wonderful.

But this is not true of the spiritual world. The spiritual world is, even now, at the apex of absolute perfection, so that there is no law in the cosmos through which anything could be added to the completeness of that world.

However, the spiritual world, even though it appears to be the very reverse of the external world, is not a thing apart. It is not a universe that exists beyond or away from the physical or external universe. The spiritual world is, in truth, the very soul of the external world, and therefore is present everywhere. But it cannot be found by going up, so to speak, in the scale of development, nor can it be found by entering the invisible, because the invisible spheres are also in the external.

We can find the spiritual world only by entering into the spirit of the within; and spirit is neither visible nor invisible — spirit is neither high nor low in the scale — spirit neither changes nor disappears, but always is what it is — the All in All.

This being true, we find the fife and the principle of spirit everywhere, in every quality, in every manifestation, in every expression; and for an illustration, we may consider the spirit of music. We know that music, as generally appreciated, is an external expression, involving harmonies of tone; but that expression has a source in what we speak of as the soul of music. And we know that whenever we enter into the soul of music, or enter into that state of appreciation where we feel that we discern the spirit of music, it is then that we appreciate and enjoy music far beyond previous experience.

We know that those who appreciate real music are familiar with the fact that the finest artists invariably approach the spirit of music, and also that the more deeply an artist enters into the spirit of music, the more wonderful his music becomes. We say that the music of such and such an artist has soul — in brief, it is something more than the mere harmony of tone — something infinitely more — something that can never be defined or described. And the reason for this we understand when we know that the soul of music contains within itself all the music of existence; that is, so much music that it would not be possible to add to its volume, quantity or quality in any form or manner.

In this very place we will make a great discovery, if our minds are open to the higher and the greater. We will discover the secret of becoming a great or a wonderful musician; and this secret consists of the power of entering into the soul of music instead of simply performing in the external. We know that an artist invariably gives expression in the without to what is felt in the within; and therefore, if the artist can enter so deeply into the spiritual within of the soul of music that the real divine source of music is felt and discerned, we understand that such an artist would naturally give expression to music that would be far superior to anything we had ever heard before. We know that there are any number of musicians who are technically perfect in their expression, but there are only a few who reveal the real spirit of the Great Symphony.

However, if all these musicians who are technically perfect would realize that music has soul, or that there is a spiritual world within the tangible world of music, and then try and become conscious of that spiritual world so as to feel and realize the marvels, the wonders and the indescribable beauty of music as it is in its sublime perfection — if our technically perfect musicians would take such a course, we can well imagine what the music of the future would be.

We may examine any art or any quality in life, and we will discover the same principle. To illustrate again, we may take human character, and we shall find that certain characters are strictly proper in their conduct and in their relationship with human life, but there is something about their conduct that appears to be purely mechanical, and therefore they produce no special impression upon those with whom they come in contact. But occasionally we meet characters who have *soul,* and we are aware of the fact that they are not only living in harmony with the great laws of life, being true to the truth in all their actions and expressions, but in addition they are giving soul not only to everything they do, but they are also giving soul to their very presence, so that when we find ourselves in the presence of such characters we are wonderfully impressed with the beauty, and we might say divinity, of the life that is being expressed through them.

We meet the same conditions in the human mind, and also in the various faculties of the mind. Some minds are brilliant, but are purely mechanical in their brilliancy, while other minds add what we might call a "finer touch" to every thought or expression; and the reason is that such minds are in touch with the soul of life — such minds are becoming conscious of the spiritual world existing everywhere, within the mind, within all things.

In any individual mind we may find certain faculties that are spiritualized, so to speak, while the other faculties remain purely material; and the reason is that the majority of those faculties have not been sufficiently developed to discern or express the soul of mentality, while one or a few of these faculties may have received such development. That is why certain individuals sometimes are so extraordinary and so superior along one or a few fines of expression, while very ordinary or even inferior in every other respect.

Thus we appreciate the importance of training the entire system to give expression to the life and the power of the spiritual world that permeates all things; but again we cannot find spirit by trying to go up into the invisible, as so many have tried to do; but only by directing consciousness upon that wonderful state within where everything is changeless, absolute, complete, containing eternally the All in ALL.

Illustrating further, we find this same wonderful principle revealed in our idea of the beautiful. We may think that we appreciate the beauty of things, and yet our appreciation may be insignificant compared with what it might be if we were conscious of the *soul* of the beautiful everywhere.

The more we analyze the subject, the more perfectly we realize that within everything that is beautiful, or back of every expression of the beautiful, we shall find the real soul of the beautiful, and this soul is *infinitely beautiful;* that is, the soul of the beautiful involves so much of the beautiful, and to such a wonderful degree, that it can only be described as infinitely beautiful — beyond all thought or expression in its splendor and glory.

We find the same to be true of the ideal; that is, we shall find that every ideal has soul, and that the ideal of the soul is infinitely higher than the ideal itself. Therefore, if we would learn to approach the soul of every ideal, we should find that our ideals would become higher and higher eternally; and we know that the higher our ideals ascend, the higher we shall rise, not only in life, but also in expression and true spiritual attainment.

In our personal development, and especially in the development of the powers or talents of the mind, we shall find in this connection a most practical idea. Briefly stated, if you have a certain talent, and know that that talent is but a partial expression of an interior or spiritual talent which is so wonderful that it contains within itself the absolutely limitless, you are on the verge of a wonderful experience in development. You realize, in the first place, that the more deeply conscious you become of the limitless and infinitely perfect talent within you, the more you express from the within through the external manifestation of your talent. You thereby not only give your external talent soul and spirit and a greater measure of life and power, but you continually bring forth into the external an ever-increasing measure of talent, so that in the course of time the external expression of your talent will necessarily become prodigious. But again, we shall have to remember that we cannot find the spirit of anything unless we direct our minds towards the *spiritual within* and recognize the great truth that in the spiritual within we shall find the All in All.

We may apply the same principle in personal development along any line, or with reference to any quality or any power, or any possibility we may possess. Within them all we shall find the spirit, or the soul, or the spiritual world; and the more deeply conscious we become of the perfection and the limitlessness of the spirit within everything, the more we shall express through everything; and this is especially true of life itself, the greatest and most wonderful gift that the individual has received from the Supreme.

The majority, however, live their life in the external, almost unconscious of the spiritual source, and therefore they never realize the life more abundant. But the moment we begin to become conscious of the inexhaustible life in the great within, or discover the very spirit of life itself — the very moment we meet this experience, we find that the gates are ajar, and we proceed to enter a state of existence that is infinitely larger, more wonderful and more desirable than anything we have ever experienced before.

In other words, when we enter the spirit of life, we find that we become conscious not only of life in its highest and most wonderful state of being, but we also become conscious of limitless, inexhaustible life — the glory and splendor of which the illumined soul, in its master state, alone may behold and understand.

For the purpose of illustration, we may again consider the quality of health; and we find that the principle of health in itself is in truth the spirit of health, or has its origin and existence in that something that we may define as real and unchangeable and invincible health — a state or spirit that contains health to such a perfect degree that it would not be possible for anything to contain health to a more perfect degree; and furthermore, that the health of the spirit is so powerful that it could not be changed or removed by any power in the external world with which it might come in contact.

If we could realize absolutely such an idea of health, we understand what a difference we would experience in our possession of health. The majority feel that they have reasonably good health, but have no idea as to what the ideal of absolute health might signify, nor do they for a moment think that there is a deeper and a finer state of health which constitutes in itself the perfection of health. Accordingly, the majority are in a condition where their health is not fully established, and frequently their possession of health is limited or uncertain.

With this condition we may well compare that consciousness of perfect being into which we enter when we realize that we possess, within ourselves, a principle or spirit of health that is absolutely perfect and complete; and having made this comparison, we will inquire as to how we may pass from the condition of the former to the consciousness of the latter. The answer is this, that when in search of health, and we all are in search of more health, we must begin with the realization of the great truth that the source of absolute health is found in the spiritual world, that wonderful state of being that exists everywhere and that permeates all things. Furthermore, we must realize that health itself is spiritual; that is, real health, which is experienced by the few as compared with the limited expressions of health, which is experienced by the many.

When we understand that real health is spiritual, and that such a state of health contains so much health and such perfect health that it could not be increased or improved upon in any form or manner, and then proceed to enter into the consciousness of the spirit of real health, we understand fully that the expression of health throughout our entire system will steadily increase until in time the personality will become so powerful with the real spirit of health that it would be immune under every circumstance.

For further illustration, we may consider the attitude of peace, or the consciousness of the serene; and although many have the power to become peaceful and quiet to some degree, nevertheless there are only a few who ever become conscious of the peace that passeth understanding. The reason why is this, that real peace is spiritual, existing only in the consciousness of the spiritual world, a world into which the mind may enter only as spirituality is developed.

When we understand that the peace that passeth understanding is so perfect and so deeply calm that it possibly could not contain higher or finer or more perfect elements of peace, we have an ideal of the consciousness of peace that is so wonderful that we shall have to think for days and weeks and months upon its possibilities before we can really comprehend its full significance.

In like manner, we may consider the state of harmony; and we shall find that what the majority call harmony is not real harmony itself, but just a limited expression of concordant activities. If we would experience real harmony, we must enter the spirit, because such harmony is spiritual, and exists only in the spiritual world. Accordingly, real harmony is so complete and perfect in itself that it could not become more harmonious.

Here again we have an ideal that deserves deep and sublime thought; and we shall find that the more we think of real harmony as existing in its perfect state in the spiritual world, the more harmonious we shall become in thought, life, feeling and action until we shall have gained remarkably in this direction.

When we consider these various qualities or states of being, we find invariably that in reality they are spiritual; and as we trace them out to their source and origin, we invariably enter the spiritual world, that world in which every quality or state of being is so perfect and so complete and so ideally placed, in its own existence, that it could not be improved upon in any form or manner.

We may trace any quality in the same way; and if we try to find that quality in its perfect state, we invariably enter the spiritual world; and here we begin to understand what we mean by the term "spiritual." It is not a state of invisibility, or something that is beyond the external merely; but it is that world in which all things are perfect and complete, wherein nothing can be added or taken away — a world that exists in all things, and surrounds us everywhere, *permeating everything,* from the simplest of the visible to the highest and the most marvelous of the invisible.

When we look into the soul, or into the inner life, we find this spiritual world established there as it is established in every entity; and we find all the qualities of life existing in the soul in a spiritual state, that is, absolutely perfect and complete; and when we ask ourselves what we really know about the spiritual world, we shall find the answer in those experiences that we have enjoyed while the mind took wings, so to speak, and we transcended the incomplete and entered into the realization of things as they are in the perfect — in the sublime — in the real spirit of all that is.

To state it differently, whenever we have experienced a joy that we might describe as the fullness of joy, or a state of harmony that we might describe as the fullness of harmony, or a state of health that we might describe as the fullness of health, or any state that we might describe as the fullness thereof, we have been conscious of the spiritual world.

Therefore, it is not what we may speculate concerning the invisible that gives us the key to the spiritual world, but what we become conscious of in that realm of being wherein all things are eternally perfect, absolute and divine. And the word "divine" may be employed only when referring to qualities or states of being that contain so much of their own reality that they could not contain any more; that is, they are, in truth, the *fullness* of their own nature.

Therefore, perfect health, or the fullness of health, is divine health. Likewise, perfect joy, or the fullness of joy, is divine joy; and perfect music, or what we may describe as the full expression of harmony through music, would be divine music. Briefly stated, perfect expressions of anything in nature, are divine expressions, provided we use the term "perfect" as implying the fullness of expression, realizing that the fullness of anything is all there is of that particular thing — a statement that becomes too large for objective comprehension when we realize that the *all* of anything is limitless.

When we develop spiritual consciousness, we may take many journeys into this inner world, either into our own interior nature, or into the spirit of everything existing in nature; and we shall find that the spirit of a flower is as much a part of the limitless spiritual world as is the spirit of our own soul. In brief, the spirit of everything does exist in the spiritual world, and is a part of the spiritual world, just as a drop of water in the sea is a part of the sea itself, no matter where that particular drop may be found.

Wherever we may turn our attention, therefore, if we go *into the spirit* of the thing itself, into life itself, into harmony itself, into peace itself, into music itself, into art itself, into any quality as it is in itself, we shall meet the spiritual world, the world in which all things exist in their fullness — without limitations or imperfections or incompleteness in any mode or manner.

Realizing this important truth, we may learn infinitely more about the spiritual world if we will continue to seek for the *real source* of every quality, or expression, or manifestation of which we may be conscious.

To illustrate: When we try to be peaceful, we should turn our attention towards the spiritual within, and try to realize the great eternal calm. In like manner, whenever we try to be harmonious, we should turn attention to the spirit of harmony, and try to experience more and more of that state of harmony that is so wonderful that it could not possibly be more harmonious. Then when we think of health, we should, instead of thinking about the body, turn attention to the spirit of health, which exists in the soul, or in the spiritual world, permeating all things.

We know that the majority, when in search for health, think too much about the body, believing that health has its origin and expression in the body only; but this is not the truth. We know that it is well to care for the body in the best manner possible, to follow all the laws of life on the physical plane and be in perfect harmony with nature as manifested either mentally or physically; but when we think of real health, or go in search of real health, we should realize that health itself does not have its origin in the body. Real health has its origin in the spirit of health, and the spirit of health abides in the spiritual world.

Accordingly, the more deeply we enter into the consciousness of the spirit of health, the more perfect and more powerful will become the expression of health through the mind and body, because when we find the limitless source of any expression, the expression itself will increase more and more as we become more deeply conscious of that source.

Here we should remember the great law — *whatever we become conscious of in the within, that very thing we will manifest in the without.*

When we are in search of power we must realize that the source of power is not found in the physical world, nor even in the mind. The source of power is found in the spirit of power which exists in the spiritual world; and if we will search in that direction we will not only find greater and greater power, but we will, at the same time, develop our spiritual consciousness, so that we may become better equipped for the finding of the spiritual source of anything that we may desire in life. This is clearly evident, because as we become more and more conscious of real power in the spiritual world, we will not only grow in power, but also grow in the consciousness of the spiritual world itself, which is indeed our purpose, whatever our external object at the time may happen to be.

Our one continuous aim, therefore, in this study should be to find more and more of that wonderful something that exists back of, or within, or at the source of all things; that is, the spiritual world itself — not a world that we may define as something finer than the physical — not an invisible world merely, but a state of being existing within everything, back of everything, beyond everything, and containing the *fullness* of everything.

When we consider the term "in all its fullness," we may well ask ourselves if we really appreciate its vast significance. We may repeat this expression "in all its fullness" again and again, in our own mentality, trying to comprehend everything that it might imply; and the more we think of it, the more vast and more wonderful it becomes. And when we realize that any quality or state of being becomes spiritual only when it appears in all its fullness, we begin to understand, not only the real meaning of the term "spiritual," but what an immensity that term represents; and not only immensity, but degrees of perfection beyond degrees of perfection, going deeper and higher perpetually into infinity.

When we pause to consider life in all its fullness, joy in all its fullness, health in all its fullness, harmony in all its fullness, power in all its fullness, wisdom in all its fullness — when we pause to consider all these things, we realize that we are in the presence of wonderful ideals; and the more deeply we enter into the consciousness of those ideals, the more closely we approach the spiritual world, until finally we enter into the full significance of the spiritual world.

The pathway to the spiritual, therefore, is not as difficult as we have thought in the past, although it implies everything that is ideal and wonderful and marvelous. The moment we begin to take our spiritual journey upon this path we realize that we are in the presence of elements and possibilities that are too vast, too immense and too sublime for the outer mind to comprehend; but we know that so long as we continue to search for the fullness of things, or to enter into the consciousness of the spirit of things, we are upon the straight and narrow path; that is, the path that leads directly, without wavering or turning, into the full consciousness of the spiritual.

In consequence, we should no longer think of the invisible, or any phase of the invisible, when we are in search of the spiritual; but should, instead, think of the perfect, the complete, the absolute, and that state in which everything exists *in all its fullness* — a state where life is so perfect that additional life could not be added; where peace is so perfect and so deeply calm that it is beyond all understanding; where light is so brilliant that it could not become more brilliant; where harmony is so perfect that it could not become more harmonious; where all the elements of life, consciousness and being are so wonderful and so divinely ideal that they could not become more wonderful or more ideal — this is what it means to be spiritual; and as we grow into this deeper and finer and higher understanding of all things, it is then that we develop real spirituality.